In Bloom

poems by

John Spiegel

Finishing Line Press
Georgetown, Kentucky

In Bloom

Copyright © 2024 by John Spiegel
ISBN 979-8-88838-461-9 First Edition
All rights reserved under International and Pan-American Copyright Conventions. No part of this book may be reproduced in any manner whatsoever without written permission from the publisher, except in the case of brief quotations embodied in critical articles and reviews.

Publisher: Leah Huete de Maines
Editor: Christen Kincaid
Cover Art: Gabe Pyle (Gabe Pyle Illustration)
Author Photo: Michael Bashaw (Michael Bashaw Photography)
Cover Design: Elizabeth Maines McCleavy

Order online: www.finishinglinepress.com
also available on amazon.com

Author inquiries and mail orders:
Finishing Line Press
PO Box 1626
Georgetown, Kentucky 40324
USA

Contents

Week 16: Child Can Hear Voices 1

Notes to Self 2
Week 30 3
Ode and Elegy to a Hometown 4
My Youth? 5
Time and Fire—Haibun 6
Things I Long For: 7
Week 38 8
Beginnings of April 9

Notes to Self 10
Day Moon 11
Ode to The Black Forest 12
In Bloom 13
On the Way to the Hospital: 14
Let the Future Begin This Way: 15

Notes to Self 16
November 17

Notes to Self 26
20 October 27
Ex Nihilo 28
They Say You See Faces Now 29
Do You Feel Your Age? 30
Lion of Lucerne 31

Notes to Self 32
Sleep Regression 33
Pillar of Light 34
Committed a sin last night, ... 35
Daylight Savings Time 36
Things I Know 37
On the Airplane Home 38
I Had A Dream 39

Notes to Self 40
Underwear Drawer 41
Out of the Blue 42
12 January 43

At the Columbus Zoo 44
First Melt—Haibun 45
Sandpiper.. 46

Notes to Self 47
Walk on the First Day of Summer.. 48
My Peach Tree Has A Disease.. 49
Tell A Daughter.. 50
Sitting at Sunset 51
Stop Belonging.. 52
Childhood's Home 53

Notes to Self 54
Counter-Clockwise 55
You don't know it,.. 56
Your First Time at the Ocean 57
Childhood's Questions.. 58
"Where to?" 59
March 25—Haibun 60

Notes to Self 61
White Frame 62

Acknowledgments

For Courtney

Week 16: Child Can Hear Voices

It's simple, really, this game we play:

I press on your mother, you wave back,
Lord willing. She says you stop
moving when I get there.

And if I'm honest, T, it scares me
how frequently you don't kick. She sits on the
couch, gasps for an instant, before I can move.

But I'm sure you don't know
exactly what's pressing down,
pushing in;

I wonder if you know I'm there,
nudging. I want voice, touch—
sibilance, nerve endings.

I'm told holding you to my chest,
no shirt, will encourage a closeness
between us;

it's scary to need help,
to need something other than
what I have, what your mother has;

I know
this wall of skin and time will
soon be gone,

it's true. But under all this pressure,
this doubt pushing down on me,
I can't help but push back.

Notes to Self

Bags packed for the hospital
will be missing something: diapers,
books to read, a change of clothes. If not the items, the bag
itself. Adjusting a car seat is a two-person task.
Time doesn't exist
in the maternity ward.
You don't exist
in the maternity ward.

Week 30

You're not more patient than us. No,
You're just smaller. Yes, maybe more content.

Or you can't hear us call, no.
We call your name. Yes. But you don't know it yet, you don't respond, or can't.

It all feels the same out here,
when we do feel. When we do know.

So we're waiting. Yes.
Counting fingers. Yes.
But we're still scared.

Ode and Elegy to a Hometown

Wexley, as it was called, became New Albany.
In the 90s, model homes and links courses
replaced cornfields,
homes at least 2 stories.

Riding my bike down the development,
I climbed cracked slabs, searched
concrete on construction sites for old
fossils of trilobites.

My mother would joke that we lived
"On the other side of the white fence," and I laughed,
not getting the joke. Our back yard bordered by
a brown fence butted against a pasture.

Siblings and I skated on golf course
pond during winter. Someone called
the cops, had us kicked off. "We're going
to put up a sign," and it shouts.

In 3rd grade, the new elementary school
always felt too nice for me. Didn't
want to track mud on the polished compass rose
inlays in the hallway.

Halloween trick or treating took place
across the street: those houses could afford
better candy, worth the time of a child,
could fill up a hand-me-down pillowcase.

My mother told me many times how she used to
save for weeks to bake cookies as a child,
that she and dad would put ramen in mashed potatoes
to make it last longer, which sounded like a challenge.

My home town is a fence around space.
A white fence for 2 miles straight. Black
fence blinks. Then more white fence.

My Youth?
    —After Larry Levis

I hear it in my voice,
my father's voice, that growled
at my dog, grounded me for dumping
snow down my brother's shirt. I hear it when
I groan as a car cuts me off or
gift bags keep falling off shelves.

I see it in my students' faces, so like
my sister's face. She's a child
in my mind. And when I drove to Indiana
last night after her car had broken down,
though she'd never admit it, she was scared,
looked like she was about to cry, like a middle
schooler who couldn't find their homework might
break down next to their locker, sinking; like my
sister when she was learning to play piano,
read music, and fell hunched and frustrated over the
scraped strings and keys.

I feel it in my unborn daughter's clothes; the fleece
onesie feels the same on my face
as my blanket on my childhood bed. I
loved sterile hotel blankets and
wanted one for Christmas. It
rested on the edge, never used.

I see it in the moon, it follows me
but it always seems to spin further and further away.
When I was a child, my family drove out west, didn't stop
until late, but Dakota was still warm. The kids
flopped out of the van, so tired, so cramped;
we got only one hotel room and shared beds.
I got along better with my sister than the others,
so we would sprawl out next to each other—she still
doesn't come up past my chin.

I feel it in photographs, yellowed on the edges.
I am almost eight, angled teeth smile for the camera. My sister
is in front of me, able to sit and hold her head; I rest my chin
on top of her still thin hair, and she smiles up, watching.

Time and Fire—Haibun

The vinyl siding used to be red, like a barnside, rusted and flecked. Parents painted the old house a modern gray. How cruel time passes even when I'm not there. Driving over for Thanksgiving, I comment on the highway newly under construction. I remember them fixing 161 and it's already deteriorating—potholes and tar patchwork. There's a taco place where there used to be a bank, new apartments in the old field we threw frisbee in. I was so excited when construction finished on the Dunkin' near our new place. "Finally," I said to you. Wonder how townies would feel now that University is on break. Time is a beast with heat, and this highway and our car, the pothole and the tar all burn. Me and my parents. My memory of and in the ash. I'm not Catholic, but mourning made sense to me.

    David danced and wept,
    the Psalms say. Which is funny, calling it praise.
    Does praise burn?

Things I Long For:

long work days
when I'm not in them:
moonlight and streetlight.

Dark of a parking
lot, dark of a bedroom.
Curtains over both windows

in my old apartment, windows
in slanted ceilings. I long
for slanted ceilings no matter

how claustrophobic they make
a space. Daily trips to the grocery store.
Leaving front doors unlocked.

Long for old doors with worn
paint near the handle, a round
handle with a dent where the index finger grabs.

Week 38

My cigar smoke swims through the air,
slowly migrates with the wind, north today,

as jays and finches sing about spare
time for the journey south; migrations

always seem in progress, never seem to
end. Chinook wait almost a year after hatching

before they head to the ocean. Monarchs
float from Canada to Mexico in a matter

of months; but T, when you finally feel warm
and travel the three inches to me, will

you wonder what season it is? Will you
wish you were back?

Beginnings of April

Blade cuts grass and an ax,
silver-sharp, hacks and splits.
A gopher we named Frank digs
fresh holes in the dirt, ground,
unstable topography. I've heard
that the smell of a freshly cut lawn is
a stalk's distress signal, a cry
for help.

Levi, a man I met in Lucerne,
let his dog wander by the city gate as he glanced
at rooftops. He walked slower than I did,
had waxed and twirled his mustache.
He seemed comfortable
walking silently, with his dog
wandering by the short grass
near the wrought iron fence
along the watchtower city walls.

Notes to Self

Our child will be a sum of
the two of us. For better or worse.

People rarely play the villain
on purpose. I might be the same obstacle

I want my child to overcome. Trouble follows
families. My great-grandfather passed when

Grandpa Jack was 3. Dad said "I love you"
through ice cream and coffee.

I'm worried I won't know enough to be a father.
How do I play with a child? Do I always smile

at her? Will she know what to do with a rattle?
When she reaches to be held, how long do I wait

to pick her up? A child feels this uncertainty.
Some 2nd law or instinct.

Day Moon

You blend into the background like a
linden leaf against grass,
round and full. You are a day
moon. A ring of condensation around
my mug, proof that something rested here.
Like a lamp in the daylight,
you obscure my view of the sunset;
You're still there for the sunrise.
Most days, you're brighter than the sun.
It has been January for months now. Lunar cycles
don't apply here. The tide is always coming in.
Once a new moon, slowly growing more full.

Ode to The Black Forest

My family tree traces back
here, grows in Germany where sheep climb
the mountain that shades me, makes
my breath visible despite the high sun.
Deer Jump river to our north; students ask
to be in my poem and I shirk the question
while looking past them at the shallow, white water.
Moss turns the tile roofs green with age. In Hell's Valley,
roads and rails make capillaries through the capped
mountains I rest on. Even hiking through the forest,
over wooden bridges and worn down stone steps. Stepping
gently on leftover snow compacted into ice. After a grandparent
slipped and broke an ankle, you kept growing, roots going
down, branches searching for sun.

In Bloom

When I wait outside long enough
the deer will come out
and act like I'm
not there,

as if I were no more than a tree,
and I were in bloom
just like everything
else.

When the cottonwood trees
shed their seeds in
mid-June, it looks
like snow.

Deer graze among
the fields, their snouts
look like my dog's
in winter.

On the Way to the Hospital:

Dorothy Ln. left turn closed for construction;
I never go this far west of town.

So many stores I've never seen before,
that one Nirvana song playing quietly.

Driving feels different at 4:30 A.M.
Dead skin where my lip split that I

chew to keep from singing.
Handy One's Liquor and Sure Shots bar,

which sounds like a gun store to me.
You've been up since 2.

My students thought we were "seducing"
labor, and that wasn't supposed to be until

this evening. Brackston Hicks? At a light I say
I didn't wake up this early just to get sent home,

and the humor falls flat. You go to the 4th floor,
I park—C2 garage—and walk upstairs,

glance at the lobby piano. I used to play,
or at least fake it. I memorized music,

never truly read. I've forgotten so much,
or never learned, which is really the same thing.

Let the Future Begin This Way:

The Mother and Baby wing
of a hospital rests
in the key of contentment.

I sleep without needing noise
or a distraction, and I wake up
to my alarm, not three minutes
or hours before. My alarm rings

in the key of energy. I am hydrated,
drink water more often than I drink
coffee. Scripture says water is God's gift
of life, that He's a water which keeps

us from going thirsty. My ankle doesn't crack
when I walk, old injuries heal.
I write about something other than sleep;
I enjoy writing and like what I write.

Not out of obligation or because
there's some alien thought trying to find
its way out. Books don't go unfinished,
and the accordian is popular

with people other than buskers. Bricks don't crumble
under wear, and weeds don't grow through cracks
in the road that don't exist. God's streets are made
of gold, not concrete. And I wonder if gold gets potholes.

We manually drive our self-driving cars because it's leisure
time—even in emergencies; it helps us feel
in control. And as we arrive at the hospital,
laboring, you breathe. And you breathe.

And too much light doesn't hurt my eyes
or make me feel tired, but in the future,
I'm sure light won't really be made of light.

Notes to Self

Congratulations come first,
then tales of how life changes,
how you have less time or memory
for yourself or of.
"We're busy. We have a lot on our mind," you might say.
"Just you wait," they may say and laugh as
if they're the first to make the joke.
A cliché meant well, but doesn't
make you more excited to have children. Only serves
as a glimpse into their life, how unhappy
they might be, how they try to hide it, how cliché
doesn't distill an emotion, it waters it down.
Overwaters it.

November

1

It's been raining since morning;
water drips through ceiling tiles.
I grow weary of such weather
with the weekend ahead.

Your mother fills out a baby book
while I hold you, sip coffee and Bailey's.
Dessert or necessity. Caffeine
sleep—darker earlier, sleep the same.

2

She's on maternity leave. Then teaching
math again. Long-term sub til full term. How
does one plan to be gone for so long?
How can they be her children
for so long and then not be hers?

You are already mine. This is not
substitution. Maybe addition. One
whole heart to consume. My
denominators are growing larger.

3

Grandma visits for the first time. Open big bay window curtains show the light, street
drying for the first time in days. One small birch on Burchwood Dr., oak and maple and spruce lined like children. Dad says birch trees are being eaten by stress, by long-horned beetles. Birches lose leaves when the trees die like other trees in fall. Trees fall most during day when the wind picks up; the moon rises at night when the air calms.

4

Sun in the morning
shines through stained glass,
making paintings on the church pews.

Moonlight gleams
through gaps in the leaves,
making paintings on the street.

5

A single sugar maple stands in the playground—
its leaves fall on the gravel
its yellow leaves fall on the gray gravel
like a light in a
room of shadows.

6

This rain, too, is a depression.
It falls heavy on the road.

And this city remains soaked
for far too long: fall lasts,

an eagle migrates in autumn,
or doesn't if there's no wind.

7

In the morning, the fog is
the Shekinah descending on the temple, heavy

in the evening, the air moves quickly
like your hand, or mind, or mine.

8

A student mentions a singer I should listen to,
and I'm reminded of my college roommate, vocal sampling,
modern hip-hop music, newly built homes, and
fluorescent lighting; each around since
before you. The 2000s are the 1980s
all over again. We are our parents when they were younger.
We will grow up to be our children. Their children will
be trees planted in early spring.

9

Snow on the grass this morning, so early. The sun runs out of wick. T,
this is the first snow of your life. And you weren't with me for it. I'm writing
these lines so I won't forget: This morning, on Home Rd., a car drove by with slush
pushed aside by windshield wipers. When I got to work, I stopped to feel the cold under
my soles. You were probably still asleep, but it was here. Please read this someday.

10

The song I wrote sounds
nothing like my poems.
I wish I had written one
for you, but others
say what I mean better
than I could.

11

Frost on the shed reflects the rising sun—
I hold you; I'm reminded this frost
too is a kind of glass. A tiled roof,
a window.

12

The nurses cleaned
you off, the doctor stitched
your mother up, they handed you
back. Eyes closed. Both eyes.
So tired, *I can't believe you're mine*
she whispered.
I still can't days later.

13

The snow doesn't stick this second
fall of the year. But still the sky spits
flakes melt on my windshield.

I know it's all the same, snow
and rain, just a small change
in temperature and speed.

I can't help but smile, though,
when I step outside and it all
falls silently, the air so still here.

14

I sing to you most days,
hum a note in hopes
you'll remember its sound.

15

Sometimes rain freezes as it falls. It's spring this winter. I know it sounds like something out of science fiction, but things don't always make sense. People cry because they're happy. We scream out of surprise. We sit silently because we're thinking and because we're not. Today, the trees are full and heavy again—with water, frozen on the branches, not trapped in leaves.

16

Leftover snow holds on
to the branches and hovers
in the air like clouds a little
too close, a little too real.
But as it melts and drips onto
the pavement, gravel, grass,
dirt, mud, mulch, it feels like
it's raining all over again.
I thought we left that behind.

17

Today was the first in a while we've had alone.
No relatives or coworkers, the three of us.

And, T, it's hard to explain how such a simple thing
makes me feel more full when I'm given less.

We took a nap together, the three of us, and I had
trouble falling asleep—never napped well.

Something about wasting the day. But it wasn't
just that—I found myself watching you, watching

how your breathing slowed when held, how you twitch,
grasp the air as if falling when you think we're not there.

When I finally started dreaming, I was climbing
a tree, stuck somewhere in the middle.

Rain fell from the leaves on those
underneath while snow floated up toward the clouds.

18

This church window is stained glass
Ice hanging on trees is stained glass.
My mornings,
My east facing bay window, the rainbow sunrise pours
onto my kitchen floor. Your words drip
a kind of stained glass.
This poem is stained glass.
Fireflies resting on the grass at sunset blink.
My conversations with my students,
and my students sing like stained glass.
Rain falling to the street explodes stained glass.
My time away from you, my time with you,
each of your firsts I miss—

19

The first time I fed you,
you were angry after—
some air in the stomach,
something hurt or agitated
on the way down—like
students when I guide their
eyes to the paper, slow
them down, wait for the answer.

20

My habits I hope you don't learn:

Eating pizza clockwise, starting with the current time,
Cracking my neck and knuckles,
Grinding my teeth in time with the music,
Forgetting to use people's names in conversation,
Waiting for others to say "hello" first.

21

You love motion, fall asleep
when we drive or I rock. When
I sit or stand still, you erupt.
Move, you say, like a jockey
vying for position, a coach shouting
times at a runner, *Move! Move!*
A working dad stuck in rush
hour traffic. A working mom stuck.
I am taking classes—might be
the right move, but here I am,
looking forward. Will I regret this?
Will I regret not?

22

Sitting in the car tonight,
the full moon shines through
the treeline.
Parked, the moon
moves, dancing
around light,

leaves and chimneys.
I stare at the dove
above Jesus' head, it flaps

its wings, dancing
around His wounds; the
stained glass also bleeds.

23

Thanksgiving on Friday, Grandpa
tells a story about his comrade in arms shooting a man

and getting cut across the stomach—a purple
heart for a paper cut.

Cousin fumbles at the piano, only reads
the treble clef. My youngest sister

cries because she's not technically a great-
grandchild, though she's young enough.

Thanksgiving is a week early this year,
so everything feels off. Numbers

tell me more about my day than I do;
I'm somewhere around the sun right now.

24

Your mother looks at my child photos,
before the beard and baldness, my chin
more angled. She says you take after me.
Says she sees me in your facial expressions.
So I mimic your movements, walk behind, and I
imagine your mother is looking into an infinite mirror.

25

My habits I hope you learn:

Picking every stray hair,
Stacking silverware by size,
Listening to whole albums, not single songs,
Keeping every letter ever received,
Tasting the texture of words if not their meaning,
Answering the question "how are you?" honestly.

26

Deer crossed the road
Rain turned to snow
Book pages closed

Snow shaded like pebbles
on the playground. I'm watching
from above.

27

When I was 12 or 13, I choked on a carrot. Only for a second, but long enough that I knew, felt my throat tense up, contract against the vacuum, like water fighting a dam. You woke up with a scream this morning. I've never heard you scream that way—fear as if nightmare had scared you awake. You don't know yet that you'll die someday. You don't know yet that you're alive.

28

With the leaves gone, I can see through
the limbs of the trees, see what's been

hiding all this time. A red kite in between
twigs, a popped balloon held in the limbs.

29

N/A

30

Maybe I'll remember it as the beginning of something
beautiful and energizing and
slightly out of my control.

Or it may be tiny pieces, not the whole picture. Like
pointillism close up or a puzzle
one piece at a time.

Notes to Self

When a baby cries, it might be hungry, and if not, maybe tired. It might
just be crying, because sometimes babies cry.
But it doesn't know how to tell you this.
And when a baby does cry, its mother's first reaction is to make sure it's okay.
When a baby cries, its father's first reaction is to make sure the mother is okay.
When a baby cries, a dog asks its person "What is wrong? Can you fix it?"
Its grandparents remember the noise but forget their own silence.
Neighbors act like babies never cry, though sometimes they do.
When a baby cries, another baby might cry, unsure of the reason.
When a baby cries, and you don't know why, ask the moon, she usually knows.
You don't want to admit it to yourself, but you know the reason too.
The reason has no words, but it lives inside you like a sail on a ship,
moving forward with the wind: silent, wordless.

20 October

Your birthday being so close to
our daughter's makes
giving gifts difficult.

What hobbies do you have now
that our lives orbit a new
star?

Venus doesn't wonder about
Her free time, though we might wonder
why Venus has no moons.

My love, I can't help
but think how dense
our solar system is becoming—

how planets are just moons
to a greater star, and how am I to fit
a moon in a bag or words.

Ex Nihilo

When I taught my sister
the Solar System, I brought sports
equipment in from the garage:
golf/tennis/basketball.
Uranus a Football sitting on its
side. Frisbee for Saturn's rings.
If the Golf Ball is 1 foot from the Beach
Ball, the Tennis Ball is 2 ½, the Basketball
25. I used tape measure and walked
the length of the house slowly, starting
in the living room, counting steps,
marking planets, setting their foundation.
The orange 4 feet away, the pebble
from the garden past the kitchen. Alpha
Centauri A/B should have been 140 miles
away. Too young to drive, I ran to the edge
of the yard, stuck two sticks in the ground near
the willow that soaked up more water
than I could imagine, than I can remember

They Say You See Faces Now

Though I'm not sure you know your own, lips puckering and mouth opening and
  you smiling
seemingly at random. Your hands flail and scratch at your face, and you cry,

wondering what it was exactly that pierces your skin, some biting cold, some foe
unknown, God reaching down from wherever it is He's hanging out.

But what you don't or can't know is we were smiling at you first, imitating your
amazement, waving our hands with you. *I know,* we say, *I know it hurts. Where did*

that hand come from? And to this day, we're not sure entirely how it is
you came to us—God's hand from wherever it is He's hanging out.

Do You Feel Your Age?

Stretching before a run,
joint pain in knee, some
old injury. I sleep with
the sun, wake with the moon.

So large; she walks perigee,
so close, close enough I find myself
whispering to her from my car,
asking her out for coffee, telling her how

my child has grown. Though sound
can't travel in a vacuum, and even
if it could, she might not understand
me as I can't understand you

when you babble in the morning; you remind me:
you're so young. The world is so old.

Lion of Lucerne
    —*After Samuel Clemens*

What can I add? The water isn't smooth
today, no lilies swim—just moss and algae
growing on the pool floor. It isn't quiet either;
so many people crowd and shout—even me
moments ago at my students (I'm sorry).

Cigarette butts scatter the grounds as grass
struggles to grow. Rusty fences lean
at odd angles, so tired. But secluded,
shaded, and it might be a sadder place
now. New life doesn't grow when noise does.

The spear rests in your shoulder. After so long,
a wound might heal around the shaft, seal up the
injury, become a part of the animal. And one day
the world might grow around us after the scabs
finally heal.

Notes to Self

Teething is a natural pain you can do nothing
to prevent. Some nights, she will wake,
the root of the issue barely visible, bumps of white
breaking through. And gas is a natural pain
you can do nothing to prevent. Maybe wait
with prayer and prunes and patience.
Patience as she cries at night;
letting her sleep and teaching her
to sleep are two different things—
she cries not understanding time or why
you're not there. And fear is
a natural pain you can do nothing
to prevent. Fear of being alone, of being
hungry for more than you can swallow
now or later.
This hunger is a natural pain you can do nothing
to prevent. She will want things
she may never have. She will
be heartbroken when opportunities or lovers leave.
Heartbreak is a natural pain
you can do nothing to prevent.
You will hate yourself for being unable to prevent
the unpreventable. Your hatred
is a natural pain you can
do nothing to prevent.
Though your parents didn't prevent it either.
Not that you would have wanted them to.

Sleep Regression

Car driving around the neighborhood, such an odd time. Noisy muffler.   I drink water from bathroom sink.   Up 40 minutes before she normally wakes. I'm used to it, I guess.
        Pimple on my head, sore thumb muscle. Rubber nipple. Baby bumps.
      Up at 1 and 3. Pacifier Envy.   It's a selfish kind of selflessness, doing what I love for her.   The owl shaped sound machine plays static: white gray brown noise: a matter of brightness.   Some drum set tuned to the right year. A baseball
     tuned   to the right arm.

Pillar of Light

You woke up crying
in your crib, no one there, scared
maybe. Later in the nursery your tear
fell on my arm and I thought
of the Dead Sea, Damascus, Sinai. Many
people lost and crying long. Your
pacifier glowed in the dark, some pillar
to protect. Outside was clear
sky, Polaris bright and large, an overripe
apple in my arms. 9 months is long
to be on the branch.
Fall soft not far.

Committed a sin last night,

didn't tell you I was sorry
until the morning after.
Second train since midnight
passes—you cry and I receive
an angry email. Dark. Another
night on fewer than five hours.
I found myself frustrated that
you were scared and I can't
explain why. At work, I found
half a ladybug shell. Six spots;
no wings. Might be the morning
made me sentimental, but it's
still there. The clouds bring back
the poetry of rain, and I haven't
spoken since.

Daylight Savings Time

As your body tells you, eyes blink open, arms stretch;
once last night—we've grown used to these last few months.
Nap every three hours—fewer now. Those first days were

a stream of odd hours on a hospital couch. Who tells us
to sleep in the dark anyway? We trust the sun to come
back. Its pinky promises we all break when we move our clocks.

How strange to let a number decide so much. No
mathematics tells me to close my eyes—I won't believe
every promise numbers make.

Things I Know
   —*After Joyce Sutphen*

Those born deaf often expect
the sun to make noise. It would take

that noise 5,050 days to reach Earth.
Deuteranopia affects nearly 5% of men,

makes everyday landscapes look like a desert.
Antarctica is technically a desert. Penguins

sneeze to clear salt water
from their beaks. The first humans

to visit Antarctica called penguins
"strange geese." Koalas have two

opposable thumbs per paw. Eucalyptus
becomes toxic to humans if it fully matures.

When I was thirteen, my brother
and I spent our free time on Pogo Sticks.

Montaigne would have looked better
with a full beard. Female Markhor

have beards too; the beard grows
down as the horns grow out.

Armadillos can give birth to twins.
Binary stars rarely have separate names.

On the Airplane Home

"I work as a nanny for a special needs boy," she said as T reached across the aisle for a cheerio, the diaper bag jammed under the seat in front of me. "I want to be a special ed teacher." A teacher myself, I should have encouraged her, though I didn't know or can't remember her name. She wore brown boots that her jeans tucked into. Skinny jeans? Denim jacket? My wife and child across the aisle, luggage overhead, we've been traveling since 4:30 this morning. Now I'm hungry for dinner though I feel bloated from travel. The stewardess gives T a 1-liter water bottle from the drink cart. When I get home, I plan to take off my belt (it snags my stomach hair), put on something with elastic. For now, T rests her head on my chest, sweats on my shirt.

I Had A Dream

I know you missed me sitting on the couch—
maybe it's my mother in me, can't feel
free while the fire's still hot. Like there was
too much laundry to wash, repairmen to call,
but I never felt at ease when we got
home. Maybe it's because we'll be waiting
two more weeks for a fridge or because
the house smelled like spoiled food when we finally
got home. I wake up at night more than I
admit. Even on the plane. The woman
next to me used to babysit an 11-month-old
near Purdue, said our baby made her
miss it, said she studied Pediatrics.
Couldn't sleep on the drive or the flight.
Took a tram to Concourse B; amid announcements
followed T's cry. I had a dream where,
though it's probably nothing, I'm sure,
you left me for a cruise ship, took T
with you. No doubt inspired by the flight
we were on standby in Norfolk—you took
the 9:00, I took an Uber to Newport News,
met you in Philly. Those five hours I prayed.

Notes to Self

A hospital and an airplane both have wings.
Same smiles. Same single-serve
broccoli. People hoping to be somewhere,
anywhere else. Both should be temporary.
Sometimes they aren't.   Same neck
cramps from sharp angles and hours. Charts
and plans, courses and scans and *Can I get you
anything?*

Underwear Drawer

Even though it's where we are, there are fewer memories of now than there should be—all of childhood and college and living in a bachelor pad. When I lived alone, I didn't vacuum the carpet. One time between classes, I climbed a tree on campus. My dad had a broken-down fishing boat that he swore he would fix parked permanently in the driveway; I would read in the fighting chair on warm days. When did we become these adults with these problems? Pushing the stroller down the sidewalk, we talk of interest rates and mortgages without a trace of irony. The CD I took out last year gets cashed out this May. T removes her socks as she prefers, though we never taught her to have opinions. I barely remember not being married to you. How distant those days feel. I belong more to the both of you. Where have I put myself? I find myself tucked in my underwear drawer beside a neon blue bandana and white undergraduate tassel, unceremonious the way finishing a book is silent.

Out of the Blue

Students say "it's snowing" like words
make it so. I sneak out 3rd period,
walk east through the field. Wind blows
snow so sounds of static or rain
on the leaves and trees.

Tips of grass look fake, picturesque,
texture added by cold and cumulation.
Rain is a drum compared to the silent
snaking of snow. Sea shells sound of
the ocean because air always moves. A
single flake might sound the same as
water down a windshield. So slow. So low.

12 January

Magpies fly by wildflowers in Europe and gum-tree
in Australia even though they're not related.
Since October, you and I have lived
in the same room. Pretty soon mudpies and fireflies.
Home might be homier. Ah, relation. Oh, distance.
When you leave and settle, stay
the same, please. Maybe on sandy Australian shores.
And me in mountains. Every continent has birds.

At the Columbus Zoo

Penguins swim in water behind glass,
follow fingers, dive deep, change course.
Tortoise rests in sunlight. Does grass grow
fast to his eyes? White-handed gibbons

sing their morning song, each mate
takes a part, follows the same path
each day. "All this space is mine.
These ropes and ribbons. This gibbon is mine."

Did I tell you that my family knows a judge
whose son tried to steal a penguin from the zoo?
He put it in his backpack on a school trip,
put it in the bathtub when he got home—

I think of him more than I admit. More
bravery I'll never have. Growing up,
my favorite animals were cheetahs. A catwalk
went over their exhibit. I used to imagine falling

into the pit with the cats. One summer
there was a petting zoo at the local hardware store,
and I pet a baby cheetah. Before every phone
had a camera. I have no proof, you'll just have to trust

me. Why would I lie about something like this?
It's one of those lies that makes my life
sound more boring than it actually is, like lying
about my age or income, how much I've lived or seen.

First Melt—Haibun

I lecture students while my short story rests unfinished for two weeks. Finished grading their writing two days ago, but I'm scared to hand them back—scared they'll hate me because of the letter. Letter of the law is not always followed by the ones who write the letters of the law. Students don't ask if I go to church, don't ask where. Students ask for extensions, feedback, or free time. Three months I've been waiting to hear about a job. It's not something I need, just something I want, like the house I could afford with a better salary. Snow melts across campus and my shoes watermark the sidewalk on my way home from class.
    Money costs something.
    March is still February.
    It's last year again.

Sandpiper

Words seem to simplify
moments.

It's impossible to know how my pipe
smoke dances in the wind

so fast. Sometimes wind moves
the other way, flips my
pages, and it's a nice surprise.
The crickets call though night

has passed, and it's no longer
early enough for the two to blur
together. A solitary sandpiper
rests on the telephone wires.

Notes to Self

As a child, I thought meteor showers
turned into rain. Some chickens and turkeys,

I'm told, stare at the sky during storms. Mouths open
in disbelief, they drown themselves. Each time father invited

me outside, I was more worried about cold
and wet; doesn't help that those nights

seem to be overcast. During thunderstorms, dad brought
me out to the canvas porch swing where we watched

lightning strikes over carrots or ice cream.
"See the funnel cloud? That's where a tornado comes from,"

and I wasn't scared, more in awe. Grandma survived.
So when warning sirens went off last week, hail the size of

tennis balls tinked off roof tiles, I know—I should have been protecting
you. I confess I don't know how to stop wind from spinning.

Your mother grabbed you from the crib, cradled
you in the hall bathtub, I ran onto the back patio:

felt the ice on my hands, the rain soak my shirt. Foolish,
to keep meteors in the sky, send the ice back to clouds.

Walk on the First Day of Summer
    —After Muriel Rukeyser

On the hour we walk out the door,
down the drive, the one cement slab
that stops the stroller's wheels, you sit,
blink at the wind, not sure where it comes from.

On the quarter you lean forward as we go
downhill, and I remember when you couldn't sit
up on your own, swam in newborn onesies,
smiled without knowing what you were doing.

On the half I squat down in front of you,
ask if you're ready to turn around. A Boston Terrier
barks two yards over and you talk back, kick
your feet in excitement. And I sing.

I look for a hummingbird or cardinal,
as it's time for their return this year, but see
nothing except leaves in the trees that lean
over the sidewalk to watch passersby.

On the last quarter I say this line out loud
at least 4 times to get it right—I've heard
talking aloud while working helps children
with their early vocabulary acquisition, and it's worth a shot.

On the hour I step back inside, lift the stroller
over the doorstep, wipe my head; it's been humid since the earlier thunderstorm.
I want there to be something more poetic about this moment—
instead I pick you up and we go to the living room.

My Peach Tree Has A Disease

Fungi grow on leaves and blossoms; three years
we've waited for fruit. Frost ate the bloom,
cicadas took the leaves, leaves I didn't know
were poisonous until today, leaves I'll need
to tell my daughter not to eat when she
grabs at the branches, all tip toes and

Tell A Daughter

There's too much history here. Be remembered.
"We will fade" says time. My words
a wall of stone, they say, a castle, they say.
"We will be buried" says I. I won't
rust and stiffen. Drum skins crack and harden.
A jewel is time, is a lover, is a daughter.
A chest is silence, is a rock, is music.
No melody makes rocks cry. Trumpets felled.

If not trumpets, then time, damn it all.
You will leave me one day.
Beautiful too, a smile, full faced, naked.
She will believe it, but make sure it's not all
she believes. She sees, touches, but thinks.
Tell a daughter she's a song.

Sitting at Sunset

Take the good with the early
each morning
T picks at my pants where
a coal burned through
last year when she was waiting
to burn through. The day goes,
day slows. This late, it's just
me and the trucks. I breathe
language. The sky is hollow
and the world is round. Dying
might be quicker. Loving might
be more painful.

Stop Belonging
      —After Brenda Shaughnessy

Stop belonging to me so much, hair, or lack of.
It's been years since you've ever been there.

My ankle, nasty and fractured, still cracks
when I turn or twist or twill.

And eyes, nearly blind, my glasses
from high school are covered in grime now.

My desk is never neat enough to call clean, though
I wish it were. My thoughts and desires just as scattered.

I can see my facial hair, though a comfort
like a childhood blanket to me, wiggling with each word, like

the calcium deposit on my hand, a little dot
moving along the tendons and muscles. A doctor

told me to smash it with a textbook and break it
up, otherwise it will always be there; and that's

the scary thing: that I am this,
no matter how much I try not to be.

Childhood's Home

There used to be a cornfield,

Mother would tell me. But all I
could ever remember across the

street was a links golf course, rolling
hills we would slide down

to the ice when the pond
froze over on hole thirteen,

par 3. The sand around the green
became igloos when the snow drifted,

made ramps to jump off of with
crappy plastic snowboards Mom

and Dad gave us one Christmas.
Pickup hockey with a street

puck until I caught a real one at a
Jacket's game. One year when my hockey

skates still fit, Dad made a 3-inch-deep
pool with 2x4s and a tarp, filled it

to freeze while we waited on the pond.
The whole thing between the tool shed

and evergreen. Skating there or across
the street until my pinky toe lost

feeling—bad circulation from my mom's
side. *There used to be a cornfield.*

When I look across the street from my parents'
now, I see young stalks of a different kind growing toward the sun.

Notes to Self

A dozen eggs costs $0.59 in Ohio right now. $2.25 in New Jersey. Diapers weren't made for sacks of flour. I never did, but TV made me think all high schoolers set alarms at random hours in the night. The worst an egg can do is break a yolk, and even then, rarely on the user.
"Bite sized" means different things at different times. Child Reborn Project. I read a news story about a woman in her 30s who tried caring for a robot child for a week to see if it would change her mind about having children, life-size with batteries. Chris Traeger broke a mug. Foster kids growing up were enough practice. Knew how to hold a baby by the time I was a teen. Head cupped in the crook of left elbow, as Sacramento holds Reno.

Counter-Clockwise

My parents had a grandmother
clock on the mantle. I've wanted
a clock for Christmas. Mantle's
been empty for years. Nothing formal.

Hours maybe marked by mathematical
equations or minute hands spinning on
Zeppelin vinyl. Ever since T could
sit up, she's been spinning herself

in circles with her heels.
"Anti-clockwise" some call it.
Spend some time moving the other way,
not that digital clocks do a great job

of making our everyday
time travel as tactile; time is relative,
so your ten months is all
I can remember.

A 24-hour clock with a larger diameter
would make more sense.
Though a number says less
about us than we once hoped.

You don't know it,

but I used to
put on my wedding ring. Yes,
just for a minute. I would put it back
in the box. Jealous, I guess. Couldn't
wear it for the engagement.
Not sure why I didn't tell you, but I started
yoga recently. Two weeks ago, maybe. I think
you'd enjoy it, but I'm not sure.
No. Why don't we exercise
together? Only occasional walks. Dear Fear,
I don't understand you.
What do you know that I don't?
What prayer in your bedroom, what song
in your shower.

Your First Time at the Ocean

Your first steps were screams.
Sand on soft feet, foam rising
with the tide. What were those
old-timey bathing suits called?

Like all things. Goes out,
comes back. Mermaids wear
their hair up in bee hives; the
moon puts on her bell bottoms.

Might be why mermaids prefer
the water to the harsh sand—
I stand and watch waves. Turtles
dig for a week before they see surf.

Childhood's Questions

Was that you?
Where is everyone?
Why did it get so quiet?
What's a "museum" anyway?
What's an "art"?
Why do we change our voice
       when talking to babies?
Why is my back so sore?
Why are we babies?
Do clouds make sound when they move?

Which way is North?
What does blue sound like?
When does rhythm become tone?
Why do we call it "space"?

Space is named for what it has.
Around 25 htz, or 1,500 BPM, though only elephants
       can hear that low.
Blue sounds like my sister crying at the piano
       bench because the dots don't make sense
       that way.

That cloud looks like a train. Choo Choo.
I am a child again.
I don't sleep through the night.
"Mama" is "baba" is "sheep" is "Lala"
Can we really define it?
This space for existing?
Silence is named for what it has.
We're here because we're here.
I don't know who I am anymore.

"Where to?"

Such small talk for small people.
This is a sugar-coated suicide,
this life. When did we start naming people
after colors? Did we need them to remind us of life
out in daylight? You were so small, though I confess
I don't remember it much. We were all so small,
and I'm scared that I remember that less.
My childhood felt less mine and more like
putting in contact lenses for the first time.
And this year has been one day.
At least the end, the dusk, the setting
of one long sun. Bed time always was rough,
and a cab ride home was a dream, not sleep.
Walking through my garage is pinching my eyeball,
thinking I hadn't taken my contacts out yet,
not realizing my own face looked blurry in the mirror.

March 25—Haibun

Windows down, I backroad home after class; a calf hops in front of its mother. A lamb sticks its head through the fence. Puddles after rain stream and creek their way down to the drain. Yes, it is Spring. Trees still bare but bud; grass still low but grows. Wood planks around my garden rot in half, roots from a tree I never saw degrade underground and my front lawn sinks by centimeters each season.

>Something is falling, failing,
>while the rest grows, grooms. I am
>the carpenter and the ant.

Notes to Self

I read di Prima and it dawns on me that the stakes are you.
Not myself or my anger or selfishness,
failures and fears
of failures.
And each of yours are really mine. Your stumbling
my stumbling. My life will not be
the consequence of my life. I do all that becomes a man,
but what of or from? How strange to be gambling someone
else's money. A debt
I cannot repay. What can be said?
Roll the dice,
play the odds.

White Frame

Somehow this year doesn't fit
inside the frame resting
on my desk. Empty spaces
should hold all 12 months of you.
I finish my coffee, can't remember
what came before you. Before now.

I sit and stare
past Fred Wah, should be reading, but you
drop a bouncy ball and it rolls
to my feet. The rubber thuds
against wood, faster and faster,
the rhythm becoming a note, a tone.

Holding your hand down the sidewalk,
you get distracted by the wind and
a pinecone on the concrete. A blue car drives by.
Do the squirrels know that the lady who lives there
is crazy? Someone called the cops again, and they're parked
outside her house. A year ago I would have been running
alone, wouldn't have stopped to look. Empty might not be the right word.

Acknowledgments

Thank you to the editors of the following journals where these poems were originally published:

8 Poems: "Week 38"

Milk & Cake Press: "Out of the Blue"

Open Skies Quarterly: "My Youth?," "Notes to Self (pg 60)," "Ode to the Black Forest," "Let the Future Begin This Way," and "Do You Feel Your Age?"

Too Well Away: "20 October"

"My Youth?" owes its title and first line to the poem "The Poet at Seventeen" by Larry Levis.

"Day Moon" owes the line "It has been January for months now" to the poem "Wild Pear Tree" by Kaveh Akbar.

"Lion of Lucerne" responds to Chapter 26 of *A Tramp Abroad* by Mark Twain.

"Committed a sin last night" is a title adapted from the first line of "A Sin" by Brian Doyle.

"Things I Know" owes its title and structure to a poem of the same name by Joyce Sutphen.

"Walk on the First Day of Summer" owes its structure to the poem "Gauley Bridge" by Muriel Rukeyser.

"Stop Belonging" owes its first line to the poem "Head Handed" by Brenda Shaughnessy.

Thank you to my wife and daughter, the inspiration for this work, without whom this book would not be possible. To Laura Van Prooyen, Hoa Nguyen, all of the poets in Poet's Corner, and the whole of Miami University's MFA program: I did not know what it meant to be challenged before working with you all. And finally, thank you to anyone who has read my work and encouraged me along the way. It means more than you think it does.

John Spiegel grew up in New Albany, Ohio with his parents and siblings. He lives in Fairborn, Ohio with his wife and two daughters. He graduated from Cedarville University in 2013 with a degree in Language Arts Education and his MFA in Poetry from Miami University in 2020. He has been teaching Junior High and High School English as well as teaching university Creative Writing and Composition classes. He writes poetry and nonfiction from a library desk that he built. His poetry, nonfiction, and reviews can be read in *Fence Digital, Vine Leaves Literary Journal, Typehouse Magazine, Milk & Cake Press,* and others.

www.ingramcontent.com/pod-product-compliance
Lightning Source LLC
Chambersburg PA
CBHW020341170426
43200CB00006B/460